What Is the Controversy over Stem Cell Research?

Isabel Thomas

Chicago, Illinois

www.capstonepub.com
Visit our website to find out
more information about
Heinemann-Raintree books.

To order:
☎ Phone 888-454-2279
💻 Visit www.capstonepub.com
to browse our catalog and order online.

Edited by Adam Miller, Andrew Farrow, and
 Adrian Vigliano
Designed by Philippa Jenkins
Original illustrations © Capstone Global Library
 Limited 2012
Illustrated by Maurizio De Angelis p11
Picture research by Mica Brancic
Originated by Capstone Global Library Ltd.
Printed and bound in China by CTPS Ltd.

15 14 13 12 11
10 9 8 7 6 5 4 3 2 1

Library of Congress Cataloging-in-Publication Data
Cataloging-in-Publication Data is on file at the Library of
Congress.

ISBNs: 978-1-4109-4467-2 (HC) 978-1-4109-4474-0 (PB)

Acknowledgments
The author and publishers are grateful to the following
for permission to reproduce copyright material:
Alamy pp 11 (© Jeff Morgan 05), 27 (© Janine Wiedel
Photolibrary); AP Photo p. 39 (Press Association/Dennis
Cook); Corbis pp. 8 (Dallas Morning News/© Sonya
N.Herbert), 22 (dpa/© Waltraud Grubitzsch), 30 (©
Helen King), 31 (Science Photo Library/© Pasieka), 37
(Reuters/© Kim Kyung-Hoon), 38 (Immaginazione/©
Vatican Pool), 41 (© Ramin Talaie), 13 top (Science Photo
Library/© Steve Gschmeissner), 7 bottom (epa/© Peter
Foley), 9 top (epa/© Rungroj Yongrit); Getty Images pp.
4 (Science Faction/Science Picture Co), 5 (CQ-Roll Call
Group/Congressional Quarterly/Scott J. Ferrell), 19 (Julian
Herbert), 35 (Huntstock), 15 bottom (David McNew);
Mickie Gelsinger p. 33; PA Archive p. 21 (Press Association
Images); Prof Gail Martin p. 13 bottom; Reuters p. 29 (©
Michael Dalder); Rex Features p. 32 (Geoffrey Robinson);
Science Photo Library pp. 16 (Dr Yorgos Nikas), 20
(Tom McHugh), 24 (James King-Holmes), 34 (Dr Gopal
Murti), 15 top (University Of Wisconsin-Madison), 9
bottom (James King-Holmes); Shutterstock pp. 11 (©
Vilainecrevette), 23 (© FikMik), 42 (© Ahmed Abusamra),
26 left (© Eric Isselée), 26 right (© Yuri Arcurs), 7 top
(© GRei), Contents page bottom (© Vilainecrevette),
Contents page top (© FikMik). All background design
feature pictures courtesy of Shutterstock.

Main cover photograph of muscle cell culture research
reproduced with permission of Science Photo Library
(Gustoimages); inset cover photograph of little blond
girl blowing her nose with a tissue reproduced with
permission of Shutterstock (© Holbox).

The publisher would like to thank literary consultant
Nancy Harris and content consultant Ann Fullick for their
assistance in the preparation of this book.

Every effort has been made to contact copyright holders
of material reproduced in this book. Any omissions will
be rectified in subsequent printings if notice is given to
the publisher.

Disclaimer
All the Internet addresses (URLs) given in this book were
valid at the time of going to press. However, due to the
dynamic nature of the Internet, some addresses may
have changed, or sites may have changed or ceased to
exist since publication. While the author and publisher
regret any inconvenience this may cause readers, no
responsibility for any such changes can be accepted by
either the author or the publisher.

Contents

Will tissues grown from stem cells stop the need for animal testing?

Find out on page 23!

How did a sea urchin help a scientist discover the potential of embryo cells?

Turn to page 10 to find out!

Some words are shown in bold, **like this**. These words are explained in the glossary. You will find important information and definitions underlined, <u>like this</u>.

WHAT ARE STEM CELLS?

Stem cells are cells with very special properties. Many scientists believe they have the potential to change medicine for the better. However, some sources of stem cells are controversial. It is important that members of the public, like you, understand the controversy around stem cells. One day you, or a family member, may need to make a decision about a stem cell treatment.

Like most cells, stem cells can only be seen with a microscope. This stem cell has been magnified many times.

Around 200 years ago, scientists discovered that every living **organism** (living thing) is made up of cells. These tiny units carry out the jobs needed for life. Since then, scientists have been learning how cells work together to build living things. This research led to the discovery of stem cells. These special cells aren't a specific type of cell, such as a skin cell or brain cell. Instead, stem cells act like cell factories and make new cells.

This was an exciting discovery. By studying how stem cells work, scientists knew they could learn how new cells develop. Studying stem cells would also teach them what causes diseases.

As scientists learned more, they realized that stem cells might be able to replace damaged or diseased cells in the body. Research into **stem cell therapies** (treatment using stem cells) has been going on for several decades, but there is still a long way to go. Many scientists and doctors believe stem cells could treat some of the most serious human diseases. However, some of the stem cells needed to do this come from sources that cause concern. <u>Scientists, **politicians**, and the public need to think about the advantages and disadvantages of developing stem cell research before making decisions about it.</u>

*The actor Michael J. Fox has Parkinson's disease, a condition that destroys **nerve** cells and leads to loss of control over the body. It is one of the conditions that could someday be treated using stem cells. Like many other patients and patient groups, Fox supports stem cell research and would like to see it progress as quickly as possible.*

MAKING NEW CELLS

There are different types of **stem cells**. Some types are found in our bodies, such as in our blood and **bone marrow** (soft area inside bones). Stem cells from these places are already being used to treat diseases.

Most **cells** in our bodies are **differentiated**. They have special jobs to do. For example, brain cells are only found in the brain. If a group of muscle cells were replaced with brain cells, the muscle would not work. Some differentiated cells can copy themselves to produce new cells, but only a few times. They often die after a certain time. For example, red blood cells last for four months, and white blood cells for just a few days.

Stem cells are different from other body cells in three ways:

1. They are **undifferentiated**.

2. They can make copies of themselves forever (or, if they are in a human, for as long as that person lives).

3. They can make other types of differentiated cells. For example, brain cells. The types of cells that are made depend on where the stem cells are found.

The stem cells in our bodies renew and repair our **tissues** (collection of cells) by replacing cells that have been lost or damaged. For example, we shed around 30,000 skin cells every minute. These cells have to be replaced. The stem cells that do this are known as **adult stem cells**. They are found in babies and children as well as adults.

Where are stem cells in our bodies?

Scientists have found stem cells in many human tissues from parts of the body including bone marrow, blood, eyes, brain, and skin.

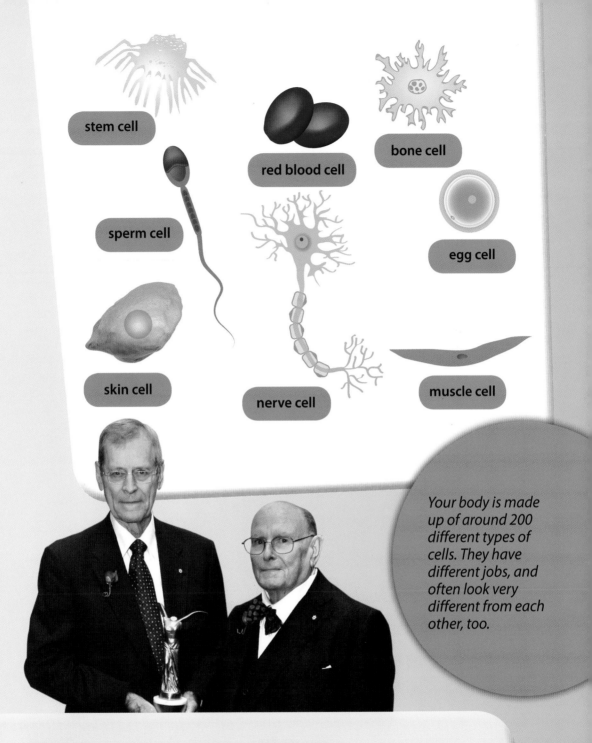

stem cell

red blood cell

bone cell

sperm cell

egg cell

skin cell

nerve cell

muscle cell

Your body is made up of around 200 different types of cells. They have different jobs, and often look very different from each other, too.

ERNEST McCULLOCH AND JAMES TILL

Canadian scientists Ernest McCulloch and James Till discovered adult stem cells and their special properties in the early 1960s. Their work led to huge changes in scientific and medical research.

TREATING DISEASES WITH STEM CELLS

Many diseases are caused when certain cells do not work properly. The cells may have a problem in their **genetic information**. Genetic information is the instructions that tell a living thing's cells how to grow and function. The cells may have been damaged or destroyed by a disease or injury. <u>A fault in one type of tissue or organ (such as the heart or lungs) can affect the health of a person's entire body.</u> In some cases, replacing the faulty cells with new cells can cure the disease.

Doctors have used adult stem cells to treat certain diseases for many years. The stem cells found in bone marrow are used to treat certain blood disorders. Bone marrow **transplants** began in the late 1950s. They were the first **stem cell therapy**. They involve transferring bone marrow stem cells from a healthy person to a patient. Inside the patient's body, they make healthy blood cells.

Bone marrow stem cells

<u>Bone marrow is a soft tissue found at the center of certain bones. Its main job is to make new blood cells.</u> Stem cells found in our bone marrow can form a range of cells, including the many different types of blood cells.

Many diseases that are treatable were deadly before stem cell transplants were developed.

For many patients with blood disorders, a stem cell transplant that has been donated from a carefully matched person is the only chance for a cure.

ANOTHER SOURCE OF STEM CELLS

Stem cells are also found in the tissues that are left over when a baby is born, such as the **umbilical cord**. This is the tube that takes food and oxygen from the mother's body to a developing baby. Cord-blood stem cells can be collected and used to treat a few blood diseases. This type of stem cell therapy is used mostly for children, because not enough cord-blood stem cells can be collected to treat adults.

Some parents store their baby's umbilical cord in case the child needs stem cell therapy later in life.

umbilical cord

STEM CELLS FROM EMBRYOS

A very special type of **stem cell** is found inside **embryos**. Embryos are the tiny bundles of **cells** formed in the first few days of a human life. Unlike **adult stem cells**, stem cells from embryos can go on to make any kind of body cell. Scientists think they could be used to treat many different diseases.

When a human **egg cell** is **fertilized** by joining with a sperm cell, it starts to develop into a ball of cells called an embryo. Inside the embryo are around 30 stem cells. If the embryo develops into a baby inside a woman's womb, these stem cells will copy themselves trillions of times to make all the **differentiated** cells in the baby's body.

PROPERTIES OF STEM CELLS FROM EMBRYOS

1. They are **undifferentiated**.

2. They can make unlimited copies of themselves.

3. They can make *any* type of differentiated body cells.

HANS DRIESCH

In the late 1800s, German scientist Hans Driesch separated the cells of a two-cell or four-cell sea urchin embryo. He watched as each cell developed into a new embryo, and eventually a new sea urchin. He had discovered that individual cells from very early embryos have the potential to make any type of body cell, and even a whole animal.

1

A sperm cell and egg cell join together to form a fertilized egg cell.

2

The fertilized egg cell divides into two. These cells divide to make four cells, then eight cells, and so on.

4

The stem cells continue to divide, forming new cells. After about 14 days, the cells begin to differentiate. For example, some will become bone or heart cells. The cells are now adult stem cells.

3

After three to seven days, a ball of cells has formed. The cells at the center of this ball are undifferentiated stem cells.

5

After six weeks the differentiated cells have started to form a backbone, brain, and heart.

MARTIN EVANS

Stem cells from embryos were first identified in mice. Human biologists often study mice because in some ways mouse bodies are very similar to human bodies. In 1981, British scientist Martin Evans proved that stem cells from mice embryos could become any type of fully developed mouse cells and tissues. His work earned him a Nobel Prize in 2007.

MEDICAL POTENTIAL

The special properties of stem cells from embryos make scientists hopeful that they could someday treat a wide range of diseases. Unlike adult stem cells, stem cells from embryos can be made to copy themselves in the lab to create millions of identical stem cells. If scientists learn to control how these stem cells differentiate, stem cells could provide an unlimited source of any type of human cell.

Growing stem cells in the lab

1 Stem cells are removed from inside an embryo. They are placed into a dish containing items that cells need to live.

2 The stem cells start to multiply. As the dish fills up, some of the cells are moved to different dishes.

3 After several months, the original stem cells have produced millions of copies of themselves. This collection of identical cells is called a stem cell line. Stem cells keep making copies of themselves, so in the right conditions they will never die out.

4 The cells are checked to make sure they are still undifferentiated stem cells.

5 Once scientists have established stem cell lines, they can start to study what gives these cells their special properties. They also study how they differentiate into various types of cells. Scientists hope one day to be able to control this process themselves.

Scientists are still learning the best ways to multiply stem cells in the lab.

GAIL MARTIN

In 1981, U.S. scientist Gail Martin was one of the first researchers to extract stem cells from mouse embryos. She also worked out how to keep them alive in a Petri dish (tool used for growing cells) so that scientists could study them. Martin is thought to have invented the term "embryonic stem cells," the scientific name for stem cells from embryos. Although stem cells from embryos were discovered in mice, scientists need to use stem cells from human embryos to find cures for human diseases. Gail's work paved the way for this next step.

WHAT'S THE CONTROVERSY WITH STEM CELLS FROM EMBRYOS?

Adult stem cells can be taken from **tissues** such as blood and **bone marrow** without harming the donor. **Stem cells** from **embryos** are only found inside embryos. In order to study them, scientists have to extract the stem cells when an embryo is a few days old. Doing this destroys the embryo. This is what makes the research so controversial.

Many groups and individuals think the destruction of embryos is wrong (see page 16). Other people argue that it is important to continue the research because of its amazing potential to cure human diseases. Scientists and other people involved in regulating stem cell research must weigh the arguments on both sides and come to an **ethical**, or fair, decision.

JAMES THOMSON

The U.S. scientist James Thomson became world famous in 1998, when he became the first person to grow stem cells from human embryos in the lab. His research led to the media attention and controversy that still surrounds stem cell research. He has said that scientists like him take the opposition to using embryos very seriously. He also said that it's a better moral decision to use spare IVF embryos for medical research than to just throw them away.

Where do the embryos come from?

At the moment, most stem cells from embryos come from spare embryos that are no longer needed by in vitro fertilization (IVF) patients. IVF is a technique used to help couples who can't have a baby naturally. Egg cells are collected from a woman's body and fertilized in a lab to create embryos. Some of these embryos are put into the woman's womb. The womb is the organ where babies develop before birth. Any spare embryos are frozen. The mother and father decide whether to save the spare embryos to have another baby in the future, to donate them to medical research (such as stem cell research), or to have them thrown away. In the United States, around 400,000 frozen embryos are stored at IVF clinics. Most will never be used for reproduction.

These antiabortion campaigners are protesting outside a meeting of stem cell specialists in San Diego, California.

WHAT IS THE MORAL STATUS OF AN EMBRYO?

Although the embryos used in stem cell research have been grown in a lab, they are just like the ones that can turn into a baby naturally inside a woman's body. Many groups believe that it is wrong to destroy any type of human embryos.

Many anti–stem cell campaigners believe that new life starts as soon as an egg is fertilized. They argue that each human embryo has the same **moral status** as a baby, child, or adult, and should have the same rights. Others argue that the moral status of an embryo changes as it develops. They believe that a ball of **cells** just a few days old does not have thoughts or feelings. It has a different status than a **fetus** (a developing baby after two months) or a baby that has been born.

A powerful microscope took this picture of a three-day old human embryo, balanced on the point of a pin. Embryos are around this size when stem cells are extracted.

RELIGIOUS BELIEFS

People's moral beliefs are sometimes guided by their religion. The world's major religions have different views about the moral status of embryos. Here are some quotes from leading members of three of the world's biggest religions.

"In Hinduism all life is sacred: humans, animals, plants, and so on. However to Hindus what matters is not just 'life' but also the different levels of 'consciousness.' In the case of this embryonic cell one may present an ... argument that at its early stage of life it has little or no level of consciousness and therefore killing it could be no harsher than killing a plant for food."

—Anil Bhanot, Hindu Council UK

"Because the Catholic Church opposes deliberately destroying innocent human life at any stage, for research or any other purpose, it opposes embryonic stem cell research as currently conducted ... We must respect life at all times, especially when our goal is to save lives."

—United States Conference of Catholic Bishops

Different members of each religion may hold very different views. For example, not all Catholics agree with the views of the Catholic Church. In the same way, not every scientist supports every type of stem cell research. Just like **politicians** and members of the public, each scientist has his or her own moral or religious perspective.

"Other [groups] within Judaism... have [publically supported] funding of stem cell research ... All agree that the Jewish value placed on the saving of a single life ... is an important consideration. It takes precedence over concern for an embryo, which lacks the status of a living person, and is available because of an abortion or because it is about to be discarded by a fertility clinic."

—Reconstructionist Rabbinical Association, USA, 2005

Creating embryros for research

In some countries, including the United Kingdom, women are allowed to donate eggs, especially for stem cell research. These either are fertilized in a lab or undergo a process to create embryos. Stem cells are extracted after three to seven days. Is it better to use embryos that are especially created for research and never had the potential to become a baby? Many people, including some religious groups, believe that this is worse than using spare IVF embryos, because human life is being created in order to be destroyed.

HOW CAN STEM CELLS BE USED?

When making decisions about **stem cell** research, **politicians**, scientists, and the public weigh the moral concerns against the potential scientific and medical benefits of such studies. These include:

1. Repairing damaged or diseased **tissues**.

2. Developing and testing new medicines.

3. Understanding better how **cells** and diseases develop.

REPAIRING DISEASED TISSUE

Adult stem cells are already being used successfully to treat a few diseases. Stem cells from **embryos** can develop into many more types of human cells than adult stem cells can. This makes scientists hopeful that they could be used to treat a much wider range of diseases. In many cases, **stem cell therapies** could replace risky operations, or the need for organ donors (person who gives an organ, such as a kidney, to someone who needs it).

Type 1 diabetes is one of the diseases being studied. Patients with type 1 diabetes cannot make **insulin**, a substance that controls the amount of sugar in our blood. This is very dangerous, and patients have to eat a special diet and give themselves injections of insulin every day. At the moment, the only cure is surgery. Several teams of scientists are studying how to use stem cells from embryos to grow the cells that produce insulin. They could then inject these cells into patients, so that their bodies could produce insulin naturally.

REPAIRING DAMAGED TISSUE

The same approach could be used to repair damaged tissue. For example, stem cells could be used to grow new heart muscle cells to replace tissue damaged by a heart attack. They could grow new skin cells to replace skin damaged by burns.

Cell factories

Adult stem cells are also being used to research treatments for conditions such as heart disease, Parkinson's disease, and type I diabetes. However, it is very difficult to grow adult stem cells in the lab. Patients can only be given the number of stem cells that are taken from a donor. More can't be made in the lab. One of the main advantages of stem cells from embryos is that they can be multiplied in the lab to grow new cells in large numbers.

Stem cells have already been used to repair injuries in racehorses. The horse Knowhere had stem cell treatment for a damaged leg and went on to win a Gold Cup race three years later.

Geckos like this one can regrow missing tails. Stem cells may one day allow humans to regrow damaged organs and even missing limbs.

FROM TISSUES TO ORGANS

In the future, some scientists think stem cells could be used to grow entire organs, such as hearts, livers, and kidneys. This would mean that patients needing a **transplant** would no longer have to wait for an organ donor.

Scientists are getting better at successfully growing cells and tissues in the lab. Growing organs is much more difficult. <u>Most organs are built up of many different cell and tissue types, working together in complex ways</u>. It may be many years before regrowing organs becomes possible. However, there have been some successful trials in which donor organs have been coated with a patient's own stem cells. This is done to prevent the patient's body from rejecting the organs.

Not enough donors

Scientists, doctors, and patients are eager to find an alternative therapy to organ transplantation (when an organ, such as a kidney, is taken out of one person and put into someone else who needs it), because there is such a shortage of donors. In the United States, 18 people waiting for an organ donation die every day.

A BRAND NEW WINDPIPE

Ciaran Finn-Lynch was born with a very narrow windpipe that made it almost impossible for him to breathe. A metal tube was used to hold his windpipe open, but when Ciaran was 11 years old this started to damage his body.

In 2010, doctors used a combination of stem cells and donated tissue to help build him a new windpipe. A donated windpipe was cleaned of all the donor's cells. It was then put into Ciaran's body, and injected with stem cells from Ciaran's bone marrow. Inside Ciaran's body, the stem cells multiplied and developed into the cells that normally coat windpipes. Using Ciaran's own stem cells stopped his system from rejecting the new organ. Doctors hope the technique can be used to treat more patients.

Ciaran and his parents after his successful operation.

STEM CELLS AS SCIENTIFIC TOOLS

The prospect of generating new cells, tissues, or organs is very exciting and could be a great addition to science. However, other types of stem cell research may bring even greater medical benefits.

UNDERSTANDING DISEASE AND DEVELOPMENT

In order to understand something, scientists need to observe it carefully. Growing and studying stem cells from different sources will help scientists answer many questions about the human body:

- How do human cells, tissues, and organs develop?

- What makes cells **differentiate**? (For example, why does a brain cell become a brain cell instead of a liver cell?)

- Why do cells, tissues, and organs sometimes develop strangely?

- What causes cancer?

- How do adult stem cells repair tissues in children and adults?

By answering these questions, scientists hope they will be able to develop better treatments and medicines that don't require stem cells.

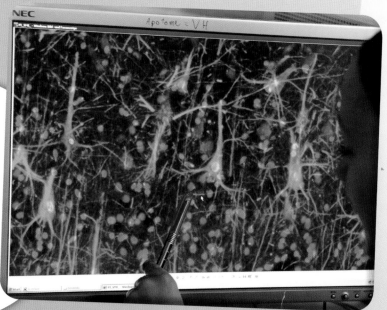

Studying diseased tissue, such as this brain tissue, is important in the hunt for cures.

TESTING NEW MEDICINES

Before new medicines are tested in patients, they have to be tested on cells and tissues in the lab to make sure they are safe. Currently, scientists use animal tissues, and live animals. They also use a very small supply of human tissue from people who leave their bodies to medical research when they die. These tests can delay the introduction of lifesaving medicines by decades.

Growing stem cells from embryos will allow scientists to produce an unlimited supply of any type of human cell or tissue to use for testing new medicines. It could speed up drug development and testing, and make new medicines cheaper.

Tissues grown from stem cells could one day reduce the need for animal testing, another source of controversy in science.

HOW ARE STEM CELLS LINKED TO CLONING?

Like organ **transplants**, <u>**stem cell** transplants have to be carefully matched to each patient. If they are not, the patient's body may reject the new **tissue.**</u> A technique known as **therapeutic cloning** offers a way around this problem, but it causes much controversy.

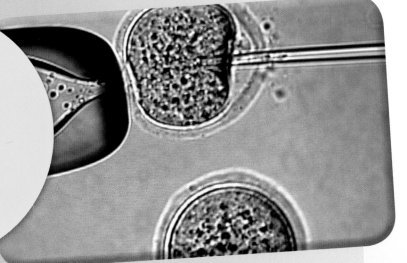

*Therapeutic cloning begins with an **embryo**, created by injecting the genetic information from one of a patient's cells into an empty **egg cell**.*

A PERFECT MATCH

Therapeutic cloning allows scientists to make stem cells that are a perfect match to any patient (see box at right). One of the patient's body **cells**, such as a skin cell, is reprogrammed, or changed, and turned into an embryo. The stem cells inside this embryo could potentially be used to grow any type of body cells, which would be identical to the patient's own cells.

UNDERSTANDING DISEASE

Therapeutic cloning also offers scientists a chance to learn more about diseases. By creating stem cells from a patient with a **genetic disease**, such as type 1 diabetes, they can watch how the disease develops. A genetic disease is a condition caused by problems in a patient's **genes**. Genes give cells information that tells them what to do. This will help scientists to better understand the disease and to design new treatments, which could also be tested on diseased tissues in the lab.

HOW THERAPEUTIC CLONING WORKS

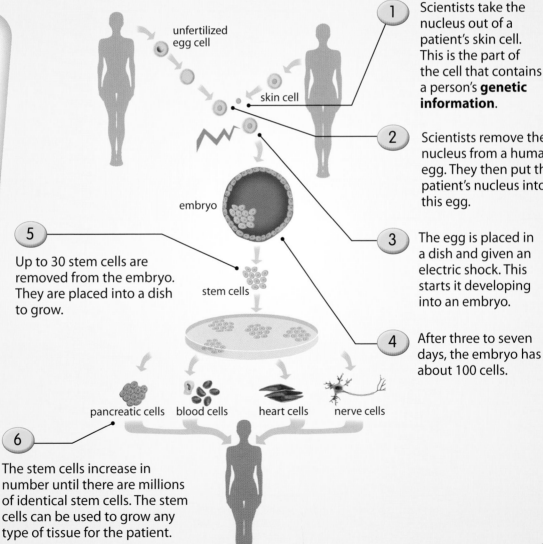

unfertilized egg cell

skin cell

1 Scientists take the nucleus out of a patient's skin cell. This is the part of the cell that contains a person's **genetic information**.

2 Scientists remove the nucleus from a human egg. They then put the patient's nucleus into this egg.

embryo

3 The egg is placed in a dish and given an electric shock. This starts it developing into an embryo.

5 Up to 30 stem cells are removed from the embryo. They are placed into a dish to grow.

stem cells

4 After three to seven days, the embryo has about 100 cells.

pancreatic cells   blood cells   heart cells   nerve cells

6 The stem cells increase in number until there are millions of identical stem cells. The stem cells can be used to grow any type of tissue for the patient.

ADMIXED EMBRYOS

Scientists have found a way around the shortage of donated human eggs for creating stem cells from embryos. Instead of using a hollowed out human egg cell, they can put the human body cell that they would like to clone inside the egg cell of another mammal, such as a cow or rabbit. Stem cells can then be extracted from these **admixed embryos**. These embryos are 99.9 percent human.

Admixed embryos are one of the most controversial sources of stem cells. Some people believe it is wrong to mix animal and human cells. The research is banned from receiving government funding in the United States. Laws that allow it in the United Kingdom have been condemned by several religious leaders.

In fact, this research is very carefully controlled. The stem cells are used only for research, not for treating patients. However, some scientists believe that other means of creating stem cells hold more promise.

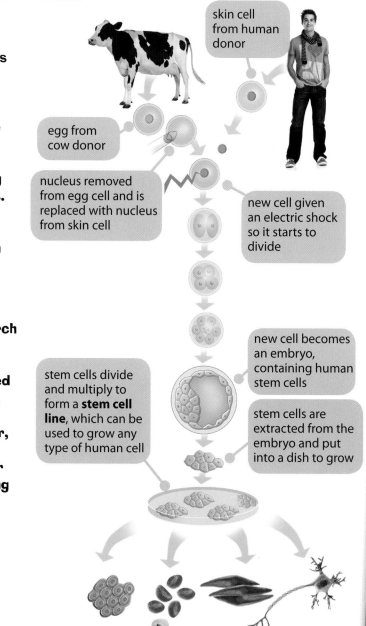

skin cell from human donor

egg from cow donor

nucleus removed from egg cell and is replaced with nucleus from skin cell

new cell given an electric shock so it starts to divide

new cell becomes an embryo, containing human stem cells

stem cells divide and multiply to form a **stem cell line**, which can be used to grow any type of human cell

stem cells are extracted from the embryo and put into a dish to grow

WHAT'S THE CONTROVERSY WITH THERAPEUTIC CLONING?

Therapeutic cloning research is in the very early stages, but doctors and scientists are excited about its future possibilities. However, the technique is very controversial for two reasons.

Therapeutic cloning involves creating embryos and destroying them to extract stem cells. As discussed earlier, many people object to this for moral reasons (see pages 14 to 16). Creating **cloned**, or copied, embryos is much more difficult than creating normal embryos. Hundreds of unfertilized human eggs may be needed to create just one batch of stem cells.

Women can donate eggs using methods developed for **IVF**. This may put women at risk of developing cancer. Some people worry that women living in poverty would be tempted to donate eggs for money.

Some people oppose stem cell research because they believe embryos should not be destroyed.

Therapeutic cloning is also controversial because the first steps are identical to the first steps of another process, known as **reproductive cloning**. This process has been used in animals to clone entire individuals. Some people worry that developing therapeutic cloning technology will one day lead to the creation of cloned human beings.

Although the media often links therapeutic cloning and human reproductive cloning, stem cell researchers are not interested in cloning whole humans. Most scientists believe that cloning humans would be wrong (see box below). However, the controversy means that therapeutic cloning research is banned or limited in many countries. Opponents say that researchers should put effort and money into developing other sources of stem cells, such as **adult stem cells**. However, stem cell scientists argue that this will delay important research, and that adult stem cells will never be as useful as stem cells from embryos.

FEARS ABOUT HUMAN REPRODUCTIVE CLONING

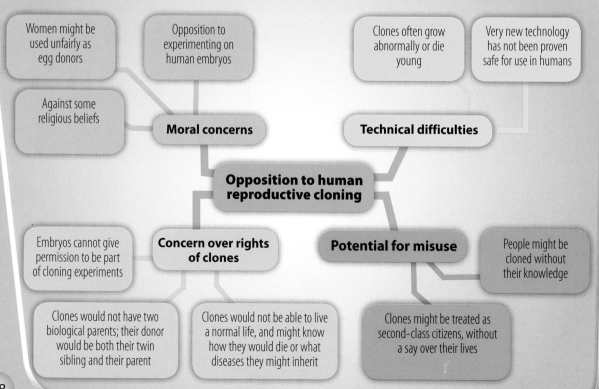

Women might be used unfairly as egg donors

Opposition to experimenting on human embryos

Clones often grow abnormally or die young

Very new technology has not been proven safe for use in humans

Against some religious beliefs

Moral concerns

Technical difficulties

Opposition to human reproductive cloning

Embryos cannot give permission to be part of cloning experiments

Concern over rights of clones

Potential for misuse

People might be cloned without their knowledge

Clones would not have two biological parents; their donor would be both their twin sibling and their parent

Clones would not be able to live a normal life, and might know how they would die or what diseases they might inherit

Clones might be treated as second-class citizens, without a say over their lives

REPRODUCTIVE CLONING IN ANIMALS

Reproductive cloning has been used to make copies of many types of animals. Farm animals such as sheep and cows have been cloned because they are very good at producing meat or milk. Scientists are even trying to clone some endangered animals to help save them. Reproductive cloning starts with the creation of an embryo from a body cell and a hollowed out egg cell. The embryo cannot develop into a baby animal in a laboratory so it is put into the womb of a **surrogate**, or substitute, mother. When the baby animal is born, it is **genetically identical** (shares the same genes) to the animal that donated the original body cell.

These European campaigners are protesting against the "ownership" of animal life.

A MIRACLE CURE?

Potential **stem cell therapies** get a lot of media attention, because they offer hope for people with diseases that are difficult or impossible to treat. However, there are huge technical, **ethical**, and political issues to consider before any stem cell therapy becomes widely used. Some scientists worry that rushing the debate on stem cell therapy will have a bad impact on **stem cell** research as a whole.

TECHNICAL CHALLENGES

Although researchers have successfully multiplied stem cells in the lab, and made them grow into different **cell** types, research into using them as treatments is still in its very early stages. In most cases, they cannot just be injected into a diseased organ, such as the heart or brain. Scientists need to figure out how to get the stem cells to:

1. get to and stay in exactly the right place,
2. **differentiate** into the right kind of cells,
3. stop growing once there are enough of them.

*Heart attacks are one of the world's biggest killers. Stem cell **transplants** would be much easier and cheaper than whole organ transplants.*

THE END OF DRILLING AND FILLING?

Several research teams around the world are looking for ways to use stem cells to grow replacement teeth. All children grow new teeth when they lose their baby teeth, but the process is very difficult to copy in a lab.

First, scientists have to collect suitable stem cells, perhaps from baby teeth or adult wisdom teeth. These have to be grown in the lab and implanted in the patient's jaw. Next, scientists have to make the stem cells start producing all the different cells that are found in teeth. Finally, the stem cells have to stop producing new tooth cells at the right time.

The hope is that patients will recover faster from this process than other dental surgery, and that the newly grown teeth will last longer than artificial teeth would. However, it is likely to be a very expensive treatment that is only available to wealthy people. Is it worthwhile to fund this research, or would it be better to encourage people to look after their teeth so that fewer people lose teeth due to gum disease and tooth decay?

People who are against using stem cells from **embryos** argue that doctors are not yet using the cells to treat patients, so embryos are being destroyed for no reason. Some stem cell researchers are eager to start **clinical trials** as soon as possible. These are tests of new treatments in human patients. Scientists hope to show the world that stem cell therapies could save many lives.

Many doctors also believe that new therapies should be introduced as quickly as possible, to save as many lives as possible. However, other scientists believe that we don't yet know enough about stem cell therapies to start using them in patients. They are worried that if the cells harm patients, or fail to do anything at all, it will lead to bad publicity. It could also cause reduced funding, and tougher rules.

Tests and trials

New medicines and treatments have to go through many stages of testing before they become available to the general public. First, scientists have to prove that the treatments are safe enough to test in people. This involves lab tests on human and animal cells and tissues, and tests on live animals. If the treatments seem safe and hold enough promise to make them worthwhile, the next step is to test on humans in clinical trials.

New treatments are usually tested with animals before they are tested with human patients.

JESSE GELSINGER AND GENE THERAPY

The tragic death of Jesse Gelsinger in 1999 reminds scientists that clinical trials should never be rushed. Jesse was born with a genetic disease that stopped his body from breaking down ammonia (a toxic substance normally broken down in the liver). Many children who have this disease die at a very young age, but medicine and a special diet helped Jesse to lead a fairly normal life.

In the 1990s, researchers were very excited about a new treatment called gene therapy. This is when genes are inserted into a patient's cells to help them work properly. They hoped it would be able to treat many diseases in the future.

When Jesse was 18, he took part in a clinical trial to test a gene therapy for his condition. New genes were injected into his liver, along with other substances that would help them work in his body. A few hours later, Jesse became very ill. He had reacted to one of the substances in the treatment. Jesse died four days later. The case raised many important questions. Did the scientists do enough to help Jesse understand the risks involved in the trial? Did the scientists rush into a trial that had not been properly tested in animals, in the hope of being the first to create a cure that would make a lot of money? The controversy is thought to have set gene therapy research back by years.

POSSIBLE DANGERS

Currently, scientists do not know how transplanted stem cells from embryos will behave in a patient's body. Will they stay where doctors put them and do what they are supposed to do? Or will they move around the body and start growing in the wrong places?

Before stem cells from embryos are widely used, scientists need to learn how to control them inside a patient's body. One worry is that they might start to behave like cancer cells, multiplying out of control and forming **tumors**, which are abnormal growths. All new therapies will need to be carefully tested in animals. This is likely to delay widespread clinical trials for many years.

Stem cell therapies promise great benefits. Should scientists continue research to find out more about their properties, or start testing them in patients as soon as possible, in the hope of saving lives?

A landmark test

Some diseases or injuries are so life threatening, or reduce quality of life so much, that people may want to be part of early clinical trials. In October 2010, the first treatment using stem cells from human embryos was tested in a person with spinal injuries. Doctors in the United States used the stem cells to grow millions of special cells, and injected them into the injured spine. The hope was that the cells would repair damaged nerves and help new ones to grow. However, the main purpose of the trial was to make sure the treatment is safe so that it can be tested in more people.

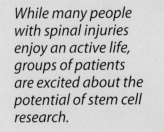

While many people with spinal injuries enjoy an active life, groups of patients are excited about the potential of stem cell research.

BETTER SAFE THAN SORRY

How do scientists and regulators decide when to introduce new scientific developments to the public? One approach is to ban or restrict new technologies if there is any suggestion they could do harm, until scientists have proved that they are safe. This is known as the precautionary principle. It aims to prevent accidental harm to human health. Some people argue that it slows scientific progress, because there is always some uncertainty in science and, therefore, always some risk.

PUBLIC PERCEPTIONS OF SCIENCE

Inaccurate media reports about the risks of stem cell research can create fear and misunderstanding. Reports that make the public think a "miracle cure" is just around the corner are also damaging. Real progress is still many years away. In the meantime, scientists and doctors warn patients to stay away from clinics offering untested stem cell "cures."

It is not just journalists who can get carried away. Scientists may be tempted to hype their work for the publicity, funding, and global fame that comes from being associated with a breakthrough. Scientists who seem to be moving too fast, or who make false claims, could make the public scared of all stem cell research. This is why scientific journals make sure objective scientists carefully review all research before it is published.

STEM CELL TOURISM

In 2009, police in Hungary arrested four people for offering untested and illegal stem cell treatments. Clinics in Barbados, the United States, Ireland, the Netherlands, and Belize have been closed for offering stem cell treatments that have not been properly tested or approved. However, in many other countries there are no laws yet. Experts worry about "stem cell tourism," where patients desperate for a cure go to another country to get treatment from a clinic offering untested cures.

ROGUE SCIENTIST

South Korea's Woo Suk Hwang became a national hero in 2004, when he claimed to have extracted and grown the first stem cells from cloned embryos. A year later, he reported that his team had created 11 batches of multiplying stem cells in the lab. No other research team had managed this, so it seemed like an amazing step toward making stem cell therapy a reality. However, these claims were found to be false. Woo Suk Hwang had made up his results. Hwang apologized for the scandal, although more than a million dollars of government funding had been wasted. But the biggest problem was that the bad publicity endangered the real work being carried out by other stem cell scientists around the world.

BIOETHICS: WHO DECIDES IF STEM CELL RESEARCH SHOULD GO AHEAD, AND HOW?

In order to decide if controversial research should go ahead, scientists, **politicians**, and other regulators listen to the opinions of the different people affected by the research. For stem cell research, these include:

- patients who would benefit from stem cell therapies

- religious groups

- scientists and doctors

- **antiabortion** groups

- the general public

Many of these groups have different points of view. Scientists, doctors, and patients often argue that it is morally right to try to improve lives by finding new ways to treat diseases. They believe that an embryo does not have the same **moral status** as a **fetus** or baby. However, many people, including some religious groups and antiabortion groups, believe that research using embryos is morally wrong. They believe that human life begins as soon as an egg is **fertilized**.

STEM CELL RESEARCH IN THE UNITED STATES

In 2009, President Obama lifted a ban on using federal government money to create new stem cells from embryos. Scientists and patient groups hoped that this would speed up progress toward treatments and cures. However, opponents are challenging this decision in the courts, saying that it breaks U.S. law.

Politicians like President Obama listen to different views on the rights of embryos. The Catholic Church, led by the Pope, believes that an embryo should have full human rights.

The debate over how stem cell research should be regulated is going on around the world.

Regulators weigh the arguments on both sides in order to make an ethical decision on whether to allow stem cell research. Does the potential of stem cells to fight human diseases outweigh the harm done by research that uses human embryos?

Regulators in various countries often come to different decisions. Several countries, including Ireland and Italy, have banned all stem cell research using embryos. Many others, including France, Brazil, and Canada, have banned certain types of research, such as **therapeutic cloning**. A handful of countries, including Australia, China, India, Japan, South Korea, and the United Kingdom have laws that allow therapeutic cloning under carefully controlled conditions. Many other countries have no laws either way.

Bioethics

Bioethics is a set of guidelines for deciding whether a type of research is right or wrong. Ethical decisions are not about personal values or morals. They are about the overall impact on the health and well-being of humans.

CONCLUSION

Stem cells could be an important part of future medicine. Researchers hope to bring new cures and treatments to millions of people, both through **stem cell therapies** and other research that can be done on stem cells from **embryos**. However, these will not be "miracle cures" that appear overnight. Technical challenges and **ethical** concerns mean that progress will require years of research and many difficult decisions.

Scientists are also researching alternative sources of stem cells, which do not involve creating or destroying human embryos (see large box at right). Some people believe that all funding should be directed toward these alternatives. Others believe that it is important to keep researching all types of stem cells to make new treatments available as soon as possible.

It is important that scientists help to educate the public about the science behind stem cells, such as through the media or science classes at schools. Public opinion is important because it influences the **politicians** and other people who regulate and fund scientific research. Also, people might one day need to make a personal decision about having stem cell therapy, if they become ill and are offered a stem cell treatment as a **clinical trial**. Scientists respect moral and religious viewpoints about the use of embryos, but they want to make sure that these important decisions are based on scientific fact and not misunderstandings or false information.

SCIENCE IS FULL OF CONTROVERSY

Scientific progress has always caused controversy. Vaccinations (medicines that protect against certain diseases) were controversial when they were introduced in the 1800s. Doctors around the world now use them every day.

iPS cells: A solution to end the controversy?

Scientists are learning how to reprogram normal body cells so they behave like stem cells. Therapeutic cloning is one way to do this, but it involves creating and destroying embryos (see page 14). Another technique turns body cells directly into iPS cells that look and act like stem cells from embryos. These iPS cells are made by altering certain genes in normal body cells. In the future, this technique may be a faster and less controversial way to produce stem cells that are matched to a patient and can form any type of body tissue.

Top Japanese stem cell scientist Shinya Yamanaka was the first to make iPS cells, in 2006.

STEM CELL TREATMENT MAP

Both **adult stem cells** and **stem cells** from **embryos** are being used to find new treatments for many conditions. Use this map to see some of the conditions stem cells may be able to treat.

baldness, blindness, deafness, Parkinson's disease, stroke, tooth replacement

heart disease

diabetes

kidney failure, liver damage, cancer

spinal cord injuries

blood loss

blood disorders

skin grafts

Stem Cell Timeline

This timeline shows when the main types of stem cells were discovered.

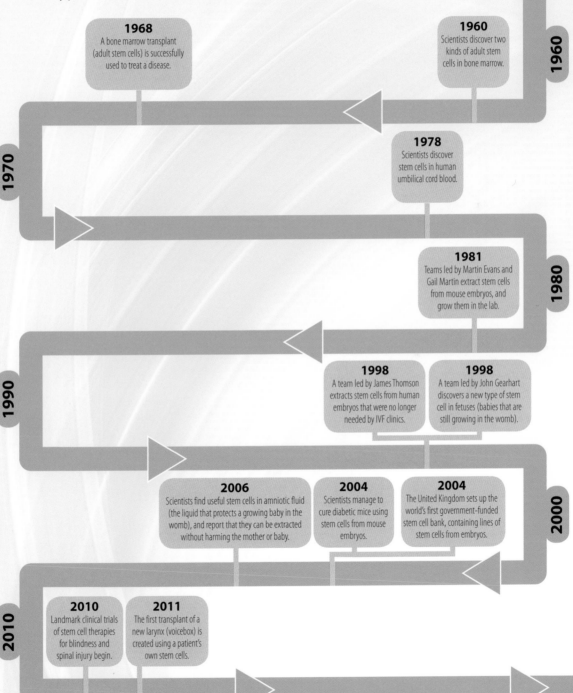

1968
A bone marrow transplant (adult stem cells) is successfully used to treat a disease.

1960
Scientists discover two kinds of adult stem cells in bone marrow.

1978
Scientists discover stem cells in human umbilical cord blood.

1981
Teams led by Martin Evans and Gail Martin extract stem cells from mouse embryos, and grow them in the lab.

1998
A team led by James Thomson extracts stem cells from human embryos that were no longer needed by IVF clinics.

1998
A team led by John Gearhart discovers a new type of stem cell in fetuses (babies that are still growing in the womb).

2006
Scientists find useful stem cells in amniotic fluid (the liquid that protects a growing baby in the womb), and report that they can be extracted without harming the mother or baby.

2004
Scientists manage to cure diabetic mice using stem cells from mouse embryos.

2004
The United Kingdom sets up the world's first government-funded stem cell bank, containing lines of stem cells from embryos.

2010
Landmark clinical trials of stem cell therapies for blindness and spinal injury begin.

2011
The first transplant of a new larynx (voicebox) is created using a patient's own stem cells.

1960

1970

1980

1990

2000

2010

Glossary

admixed embryo when a human body cell is placed inside the egg cell of another mammal, such as a cow or rabbit

adult stem cell type of stem cell found in the bodies of adults, children, and babies. Adult stem cells can produce certain types of body cells, to replace lost or worn out cells.

antiabortion people or groups who are against abortion rights

bioethics set of guidelines for deciding whether a type of biomedical research is right or wrong

bone marrow soft tissue found at the center of certain bones

cell smallest parts, or building blocks, of a plant or animal

clinical trial first tests of new medicines or treatments in human patients

clone exact copy of something, such as a living thing; process of making an exact copy of something.

differentiated cell with a specific function. A differentiated cell can only copy itself to produce cells of the same type, if at all.

egg cell type of cell found in female animals, that contains half the information needed to make a new individual. If the egg cell is fertilized (joins with a male sperm cell) the information is complete, and the egg cell begins to divide to become an embryo.

embryo tiny bundle of cells that is formed in the first few days of a new human or animal life

ethical fair, according to a certain set of guidelines or principles that people are working by

fertilized egg cell that has joined with a sperm cell, giving it the potential to develop into an embryo in the right conditions

fetus developing baby animal in the womb

gene part of the genetic information of a living thing. Most genes tell cells how to make a particular protein.

gene therapy when healthy genes are inserted into the cells of a patient with a genetic disease. This treatment aims to make the cells work properly and cure the disease.

genetic disease condition that is caused by abnormalities in the patient's genes

genetic information set of instructions that tell every cell of a living thing how to grow and function

genetically identical sharing exactly the same genetic information

in vitro fertilization (IVF) medical technique developed to help infertile people have a baby. The techniques are also used by scientists in cloning and other research.

insulin protein made in a healthy person, to control the amount of sugar in the blood

iPS cell induced pluripotent stem cells are normal body cells that have had certain genes altered, so that they look and behave like stem cells from embryos

moral status where something, such as a fetus, exists on a moral scale

nerve body tissue that transmits electrical signals

organism individual living thing

politician person who is elected to work in government

precautionary principle where new technologies are banned or restricted by regulators, until scientists have proved that they are safe

regulator official involved in controlling a particular area of public interest, such as the safe introduction of new medicines

reproductive cloning when a cell from an adult animal is 'reprogrammed' by putting its nucleus inside an empty egg cell, to create an embryo. If the animal is a mammal, the new embryo is then implanted into the womb of a surrogate mother, where it can grow into an individual that will be genetically identical to the original adult animal.

stem cell type of animal cell that does not have a special job, like brain cell or muscle cell. Instead, a stem cell acts like a cell factory, making one or more types of cells when the animal's body needs them.

stem cell line collection of millions of stem cells kept in a lab. Each stem cell line is descended from a small number of stem cells collected from a single source. Stem cells keep making copies of themselves, so in the right conditions the stem cell line will never die out.

stem cell therapy medical treatment that uses stem cells

surrogate female who carries a developing fetus, which has been created using an egg cell from a different female

therapeutic cloning when a cell from a patient is 'reprogrammed' by putting its nucleus inside an empty egg cell, to create an embryo. Stem cells can be taken from the new embryo after three days, to use in stem cell therapy for the original patient.

tissue collection of cells of a certain type, such as heart tissue or muscle tissue

transplant when an organ from one person is placed in another person through surgery

tumor cluster of cells in an animal or human body that is growing uncontrolled, without the normal mechanisms that limit cell growth

umbilical cord cord along which oxygen and nutrients are passed from a mother's body to a growing fetus in the womb, and waste products are passed out

undifferentiated cell that does not yet have a special function. It has the potential to become many different types of cells, or to remain undifferentiated.

vaccination medicine that protects against certain diseases

Find Out More

Books

Claybourne, Anna. *The Usborne Introduction to Genes and DNA*. London: Usborne Publishing, 2006.

Keyser, Amber. *Decoding Genes with Max Axiom*. Mankato, MN: Capstone Press, 2010.

Maskell, Hazel and Adam Larkum. *What's Biology All About?* London: Usborne Publishing, 2009.

Rooney, Anne. *Medicine: Stem Cells, Genes and Superbeams*. Chicago, IL: Heinemann Library, 2006

Thomas, Isabel. *Should Scientists Pursue Cloning?* Chicago, IL: Raintree Publishers, 2012.

Winston, Robert. *What Makes Me, Me?* New York, NY: DK Publishing, 2010.

Websites

http://learn.genetics.utah.edu/content/tech/stemcells/scintro/
Check out this site's fantastic animated introduction to stem cells.

http://lifesciences.envmed.rochester.edu/downloads2.html#2
Download student and teacher resources for lessons on stem cells at this site.

www.smm.org/tissues/stem_cells.php
An interactive comic all about stem cells.

www.eurostemcell.org/films
Watch four short videos about stem cell science and ethics.

www.sumanasinc.com/webcontent/animations/content/stemcells_scnt. html
This site has an animation showing how stem cells from human embryos are made.

http://mbbnet.umn.edu/scmap.html
The World Stem Cell map shows which countries restrict certain types of stem cell research.

www.wellcome.ac.uk/About-us/Policy/Spotlight-issues/Human-Fertilisation-and-Embryology-Act/Humanadmixedembryos/index.htm
Watch an animation showing how admixed embryos are made.

Topics to research

Stem cell research
Use newspaper and science news websites to search for information on the most recent developments in stem cell research. Start by typing "stem cells" into the search box.

Bioethics
Find out about the principles that guide regulators and scientists when they make decisions about controversial research. A good place to start is **www.beep.ac.uk**, or type "bioethics" into a search engine.

Stem cell therapies
Stem cells have been used for decades to treat certain diseases. Research the history of bone marrow transplants, and make a list of the different diseases they can treat.

Index